Wolfgang Amadeus Mozart

Mozart, Mozart!

16 famous selections from Wolfgang Amadeus Mozart's operas
in historic arrangements for two flutes:

selected and edited by
Elisabeth Weinzierl and Edmund Wächter

Sy. 2916

RICORDI

Preface

Wolfgang Amadeus Mozart was a superstar in his day as well as today. The "wunderkind" travelled the music capitals of Europe, and the greatest courts were scrambling for a performance by the young prodigy. Mozart became famous and the popularity of his works was eventually unsurpassed. Innumerable arrangements for domestic music playing came into being. In times before radio broadcast and recordings this was the only way to spread major works and to hear them at home. Solely regarding arrangements for two flutes, we know of more than 50 historical editions with Mozart's most catchy and beautiful melodies. In addition, numerous single pieces appeared in flute methods or collections. From this rich array of choices of historical arrangements, we've selected 16 timeless "hits."

We adopted these arrangements as little as possible and shortened them only rarely. Wherever their tempo markings differed from Mozart's, we decided to reproduce the composer's markings in this edition. However, we didn't change other aspects of the arrangements, such as being in a different key from Mozart's original music, performance markings, abridgments, or other divergences from Mozart's scores. These duets also mirror the history of the reception of these great works. They still make sense and playing them today is a fun way to get in touch with this great music, actually playing rather than just listening to it.

Elisabeth Weinzierl and Edmund Wächter
(translated from the original German Preface)

Sources for the arrangements:

DIE ENTFÜHRUNG AUS DEM SERAIL
Arr.: Anonymus. Edition: Carl Christian Lose, Copenhagen
(identical edition: Simrock, Bonn, 1799)

LE NOZZE DI FIGARO
Arr.: Ernesto Köhler (1849-1907): Progressive Duette op. 55 (1890)
Arr.: Louis Drouet (1792-1873): Method of Flute Playing (1830)
Arr.: Anonymus. Edition: Simrock, Bonn (1799)

DON GIOVANNI
Arr.: Kaspar Kummer (1795-1870): Anweisung zum Flötenspiel op. 106 (1844)
Arr.: Louis Drouet (1792-1873): Method of Flute Playing (1830)
Arr.: Ernesto Köhler (1849-1907): Die Zauberflöte

COSÌ FAN TUTTE
Arr.: Anonym, Ausgabe: Simrock, Bonn (1799)

LA CLEMENZA DI TITO
Arr.: Johann Christian Stumpf (1763-1801). Edition: Schott, Mainz (ca. 1799)

DIE ZAUBERFLÖTE
Arr.: Bernhard Romberg (1767-1841). Edition: Simrock, Bonn (1794)

Contents

About the Operas and Selections

The Abduction from the Seraglio
Die Entführung aus dem Serail
Opera/Singspiel (originally in German), premiered in Vienna, 1782.

A *Singspiel* is a German form for the musical stage from the 18th century combining comedy and drama, performed with spoken dialogue and a sung score. All things Turkish were in vogue in Vienna in the period when this opera was written and premiered.

This opera/singspiel takes place in 16th century Turkey. Konstanze, a young Spanish woman, her English maid Blonde (or "Blondchen") and the servant Pedrillo have fallen into the hands of pirates and have been sold to Pasha Selim. Konstanze's fiancé Belmonte has been separated from them in the pirates' attack and has followed to free them.

Who has found a sweetheart (Wer ein Liebchen hat gefunden) (original key: G minor)
Near the beginning of the opera, Pasha Selim's servant Osmin (bass), who will later turn out to be the biggest danger for the abducted people, plucks figs in the garden, deep in thought about what a volatile and endangered thing love is.

What bliss, what joy (Welche Wonne, welche Lust) (original key)
This aria is sung by Blonde (soprano) in Act II of the opera. She is filled with joy when Pedrillo, her beloved, tells her that Belmonte has come to rescue them.

When the tears of joy flow (Wenn der Freude Tränen fließen) (original key: B-flat Major)
Later in Act II, Pedrillo has persuaded the warden Osmin to drink with him. Pedrillo has mixed a sleep-drug into the wine. While Osmin sleeps, Belmonte (tenor) enters to free the prisoners and is overwhelmed with emotion in the reunion with Konstanze.

How does the opera end? The escape of the four is discovered, and Osmin anticipates the pain and punishment he expects for the prisoners. Furthermore, Pasha Selim recognizes in Belmonte the son of his biggest enemy, and decides on death as punishment for all of the captives. But all of a sudden Pasha Selim changes his mind. He believes that he can make a bigger point against his enemy by extending mercy.

The Marriage of Figaro
Le nozze di Figaro
Opera (originally in Italian), premiered in Vienna, 1786.

The Marriage of Figaro is one of the most sophisticated comedies ever written for the operatic stage, and one of the most often produced operas in the world. At its heart is the questioning of the role of the aristocracy, and the relationship between the servant class and the noble folk they serve.

This opera is based on a famous French play by Beaumarchais, the second part of a trilogy. (The first part is the story of Rossini's opera *The Barber of Seville*.) It takes place in and near Seville in the 17th century (though it is custom to play it in an 18th century setting.) Figaro, barber and jack-of-all-trades, is valet to Count Almaviva. Figaro is to be married to Susanna, a lady's maid to the Countess, Rosina. The Count is making advances toward Figaro's bride-to be, Susanna. The wedding of the two servants is planned for this very day. *The Marriage of Figaro* is a comic opera with lots of masquerades, scheming and mistaken identities. Most of them belong to a set of intrigues which the Countess, Susanna and Figaro spin to expose the Count's shenanigans, and bring him back to his wife.

You will frolic no more (Non più andrai) (original key)
At the end of Act I the Count's adolescent page, Cherubino, is expecting punishment for one of his latest amorous adventures with the gardener's daughter, Barbarina, and is asking for Susanna's aid. When the Count suddenly enters Susanna's chamber attempting to make love to her, Cherubino hides—but is discovered. The Count sends him away to become a soldier in his regiment in Seville. In this famous aria, Figaro (a bass) teases Cherubino and attempts to cheer him up about the military life ahead, which will exclude all comforts.

You who know (Voi che sapete) (original key: B-flat Major)
In the beginning of Act II, Susanna and Rosina dress Cherubino (a "pants role" which is performed by a woman, portraying the male character's youth) with women's clothes so that he can stay at the court in disguise at least until the wedding. While they dress him, he sings this aria, describing the confusing feelings of young love he feels, asking for their wise counsel.

Oh, come, do not delay (Deh vieni non tardar) (original key: F Major)
Act III ended with the marriage of Susanna and Figaro. In Act IV Susanna and the Countess have come to the garden, dressed in each other's clothes. Susanna has arranged a fake rendezvous with the Count in which he should make advances to his wife, who is dressed in disguise as Susanna. However, they haven't informed Figaro about the plan, so he believes a secret meeting of Susanna and Almaviva is taking place and is very jealous. Susanna (soprano), knows Figaro is listening and teases him by singing this aria, a love song to her beloved who, in Figaro's imagination, must be Almaviva. Later things are resolved between the newlywed couple.

How does the opera end? When the Count comes, the trap snaps shut. He confirms his love to "Susanna", really his wife in disguise, and when she finally reveals her true identity as the Countess he honestly pleads for forgiveness. The Countess forgives him and the couple is reunited. The opera ends happily.

Don Giovanni
Opera (originally in Italian), premiered in Prague, 1787.

Don Giovanni is one of the oldest operas to constantly remain in the international repertory consistently since its premiere. **Don Giovanni**, subtitled *il dissoluto punito* (the punished rake), is a dramma giocoso, a genre which blends serious and comic elements. The opera is based on the legends of the fictional character of Don Juan, a libertine Spanish nobleman who devotes his life to seducing women.

The opera takes place in and near Seville in the 17th century (though it is a custom to play it in an 18th century setting.) The plot begins dramatically: Donna Anna's father (the Commendatore) discovers that Don Giovanni has seduced his daughter. In making his escape Don Giovanni kills Donna Anna's father. Donna Anna and her fiancé, Don Ottavio, swear vengeance. Then we see Donna Elvira, a noble lady who has been abandoned by Don Giovanni some time before. She also swears vengeance.

There we will join hands (Là ci darem la mano) (original key)
The seducer Don Giovanni (baritone) first sees the charming peasant girl Zerlina at her wedding procession to marry Masetto. Don Giovanni is immediately attracted to her. He manages to separate her from the crowd and begins his seducing arts while singing this famous duet with Zerlina (soprano). Despite the circumstances, she finds herself tempted by the Don's magnetism.

Beat me, handsome Masetto (Batti, batti, o bel Masetto) (original key: F Major)
After the Don Giovanni's advances are deflected, Zerlina (soprano) sings this aria to calm her jealous Masetto and to persuade him of her innocence. (She playfully says "beat me" to him, a witty and disarming thing to say to the gentle Masetto.)

Oh, come to the window (Deh vieni alla finestra) (original key)
In the beginning of Act II, Don Giovanni plays a trick on the persistent Donna Elvira, who has been pestering him. He pretends that he will come back to her. She finally is convinced, and Giovanni sends his servant Leporello, disguised as his master, to Elvira, while Don Giovanni seduces Elvira's maid with this serenade.

How does the opera end? Elvira feels more sorrow than anger toward the immoral Don Giovanni, and asks him to change his life. He turns her down cynically. All attempts by Donna Anna, Don Ottavio and Masetto to catch Giovanni fail. He even is arrogant enough to invite the ghost-statue of the killed Commendatore to dinner. The ghost-statue gives Don Giovanni the last chance to repent and change his life. As the willful Don Giovanni turns this down as well, the statue sinks into the ground and takes Don Giovanni with him. The rake is punished.

Così fan tutte

(*The School for Lovers*)
Opera (originally in Italian), premiered in Vienna, 1790.

Così fan tutte (an idiomatic Italian title that is difficult to translate) was Mozart's third opera with a libretto by Lorenzo da Ponte. Though now considered not only a musical masterpiece but a subtle probing of humanity, the opera was neglected until the mid-20th century.

This comic opera takes place in 18th century Naples. The first scene sets off a game, which fills almost the entire opera: The young military officers Ferrando and Guglielmo talk about their fiancées, the sisters Dorabella and Fiordiligi, and that they are absolutely sure of them being forever faithful. The philosopher Don Alfonso joins in and persuades them to accept a wager: He will prove in the course of only one day that the women are changeable and capable of being unfaithful. A faked letter is contrived to call both officers off to war. Shortly afterward they should return in disguise as Albanians. In playing out the wager with Don Alfonso, the disguised Guglielmo attempts to seduce Dorabella (Ferrando's fiancée), and the disguised Ferrando attempts to seduce Fiordiligi (Gugliemo's fiancée).

Do not be bashful (Non siate ritrosi) (original key)
In the middle of Act I, the two men, disguised as Albanians, have arrived at the sisters' house to try to win their hearts. This aria is sung by the disguised Guglielmo (baritone), praising with exaggeration his manly attributes as a suitor.

An aura of love (Un' aura amorosa) (original key)
Ferrando (tenor) is happy that his fiancée, Dorabella, remains faithful, despite the attempted seduction by the disguised Guglielmo In this aria he sings of his love for Dorabella.

Love is a little thief (È amore un ladroncello) (original key: B-flat Major)
The insisting wooing has finally brought some success. Dorabella and Fiordiligi have decided that a little flirting with the "Albanians" wouldn't harm their real loves. But while Fiordiligi and Ferrando don't go much further than conversation at this point, Guglielmo and Dorabella exchange love gifts. In this aria, Dorabella (mezzo-soprano) playfully confesses to her sister what has happened.

How does the opera end? The four lovers show conflicting emotions throughout the opera. Fiordiligi's resistance soon falls and she winds up in Ferrando's arms. Don Alfonso has won the wager: Così fan tutte, his philosophy that all women are like that. A double marriage ceremony of the "Albanians" and the sisters is arranged. The disguises are revealed. Everybody accepts that all what happened is an inevitable consequence of human nature, and they forgive each other. Fiordiligi returns to Guglielmo and Dorabella returns to Ferrando. (In some productions the lovers instead remain with their new partners.)

La clemenza di Tito

(*The Clemency of Titus*)
Opera (originally in Italian), premiered in Prague, 1791.

Mozart wrote this **opera seria** (a genre of serious opera in the 18th century) following a commission of the Estate of Bohemia while he was already working on **The Magic Flute**. It is reported that he finished the score within 18 days, except for the recitatives, which were probably written by his pupil, Süssmayr.

The plot takes place in Rome, 79-81 A.D. The Roman emperor Tito (Titus) is to marry Berenice. This enrages the ambitious Vitellia, who persuades Sesto (Sextus) to assassinate Tito. Tito changes his mind and declines to marry Berenice, planning to marry Servilia instead. But when Tito learns that Servilia loves Annio, he renounces her and plans to wed Vitellia. Vitellia learns of this too late to stop Sesto's assassination attempt. Titus avoids being killed, and the intended assassin Sesto is tried and condemned to death. Tito surprisingly grants him a pardon. Vitellia ultimately confesses her part in the assassination plot, but is also forgiven.

Who blindly believes (Chi ciecamente crede) (original key: G Major)
Sesto is upset because he feels as if he is being used. Vitellia (soprano) calms him down with this aria: She sings philosophically, "Who blindly believes will gather faith, and who always distrusts will gather betrayal."

The Magic Flute

Die Zauberflöte

Opera/Singspiel (originally in German), premiered in Vienna, 1791.

The Magic Flute is a ***Singspiel*** (like ***The Abduction from the Seraglio***), a combination of spoken and sung passages, of comedy and serious drama. This complicated fairy tale story was Mozart's last work for the stage. He died of illness just over two months after the premiere of ***The Magic Flute.***

The Bird Catcher Am I (Der Vogelfänger bin ich ja) (original key)

In this entrance aria sung by Papageno (baritone), he tells of his profession of catching and selling birds, and his longing to find a wife.

When Tamino sees a picture of Pamina, the daughter of the Queen of the Night (whom we later learn is evil), he immediately falls in love with her. He is told that she has been captured by the sorcerer Sarastro. The Queen of the Night promises Tamino that he can marry Pamina if he frees her. Papageno is told to accompany Tamino on his mission. Each of them gets a magic instrument for protection. Tamino receives a magic flute, and Papageno receives a magic Glockenspiel (a set of bells).

How strong is your magic (Wie stark ist nicht dein Zauberton) (original key)

When Tamino arrives at Sarastro's palace he learns that things are not as represented by the Queen of the Night. In fact, Sarastro is a noble priest representing the ideals of humanity, and the Queen wants to destroy him and his benevolent influence. Bewildered by the new situation, Tamino (tenor) starts playing the magic flute and sings this aria, expressing his longing for Pamina. Animals from the wilderness respond to the magic flute, and tamely surround him.

Tamino becomes convinced of the worthiness of the brotherhood Sarastro leads. Sarastro tells Tamino that he has to undergo a series of trials of wisdom and temperance to show that he is worthy to become Pamina's husband. Sarastro plans to make the couple the new rulers of his temple. Papageno is told that he would find a young and beautiful wife called Papagena if he would undergo these trials as well. Unsurprisingly, the simple man fails with every of one of them. He gives up quickly and asks for a glass of wine.

A maiden or wife (Ein Mädchen oder Weibchen) (original key)

Papageno gets a glass of wine and sings of his hopes again. Like an answer, an elderly woman he has already encountered earlier re-appears and tells him that he must marry her or stay imprisoned for the rest of his life. Papageno reluctantly agrees and the old woman suddenly turns into the pretty young Papagena.

How does the opera end? Tamino masters all trials and weds the princess Pamina, whereas the evil and conniving Queen of the Night is sent into eternal darkness.

What bliss, what joy

(Welche Wonne, welche Lust)

The Abduction from the Seraglio

Wolfgang Amadeus Mozart
Arranged by Anonymous (ca. 1799)

Sy. 2916

Who has found a sweetheart

(Wer ein Liebchen hat gefunden)

The Abduction from the Seraglio

Wolfgang Amadeus Mozart
Arranged by Anonymous (ca. 1799)

Edition Ricordi Sy. 2916

When the tears of joy flow
(Wenn der Freude Tränen fließen)

The Abduction from the Seraglio

Wolfgang Amadeus Mozart
Arranged by Anonymous (ca. 1799)

Edition Ricordi   Sy. 2916

Edition Ricordi

Sy. 2916

You will frolic no more

(Non più andrai)

The Marriage of Figaro

Wolfgang Amadeus Mozart
Arranged by Ernesto Köhler (1890)

You who know
(Voi che sapete)

The Marriage of Figaro

Wolfgang Amadeus Mozart
Arranged by Louis Drouet (1830)

*) Original: E♭ / Source: E♭

Oh, come, do not delay
(Deh vieni non tardar)
The Marriage of Figaro

Wolfgang Amadeus Mozart
Arranged by Anonymous (1799)

Edition Ricordi

Sy. 2916

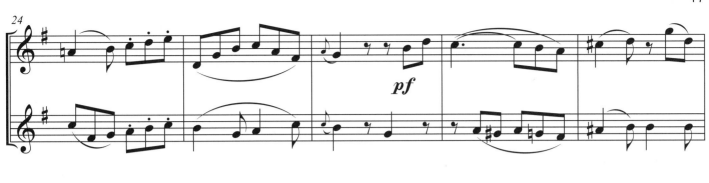

Edition Ricordi
Sy. 2916

There we will join hands
(Là ci darem la mano)
Don Giovanni

Wolfgang Amadeus Mozart
Arranged by Kaspar Kummer (1844)

Sy. 2916

Beat me, handsome Masetto
(Batti, batti, o bel Masetto)

Don Giovanni

Wolfgang Amadeus Mozart
Arranged by Louis Drouet (1830)

Oh, come to the window
(Deh vieni alla finestra)
Don Giovanni

Wolfgang Amadeus Mozart
Arranged by Ernesto Köhler (1895)

Sy. 2916

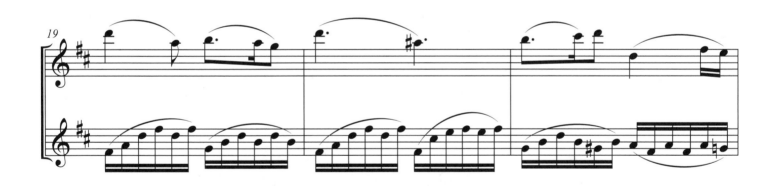

Do not be bashful

(Non siate ritrosi)

Così fan tutte

Wolfgang Amadeus Mozart
Arranged by Anonymous (1799)

An aura of love

(Un'aura amorosa)

Così fan tutte

Wolfgang Amadeus Mozart
Arranged by Anonymous (1799)

Sy. 2916

Love is a little thief
(È amore un ladroncello)
Così fan tutte

Wolfgang Amadeus Mozart
Arranged by Anonymous (1799)

*) Original: D♯ (suggestion D♮) / Source: D♯ (appoggiatura D♮)

**) Original: B / Source B-flat

Sy. 2916

© 2014 by G. Ricordi & Co., Berlin

Who blindly believes
(Chi ciecamente crede)

La clemenza di Tito

Wolfgang Amadeus Mozart
Arranged by Johann Christian Stumpf (ca. 1799)

Sy. 2916

The Bird Catcher am I
(Der Vogelfänger bin ich ja)
The Magic Flute

Wolfgang Amadeus Mozart
Arranged by Bernard Romberg (1794)

Sy. 2916

Sy. 2916

How strong is your magic
(Wie stark ist nicht dein Zauberton)
The Magic Flute

Wolfgang Amadeus Mozart
Arranged by Bernard Romberg (1799)

A maiden or wife
(Ein Mädchen oder Weibchen)
The Magic Flute

Wolfgang Amadeus Mozart
Arranged by Bernard Romberg (1799)